EDGE OF EXTINCTION

# WHALES

TRICIA HOFFMAN

PowerKiDS press

Published in 2027 by The Rosen Publishing Group, Inc.
2544 Clinton Street, Buffalo, NY 14224



First Edition

Portions of this work were originally authored by Michael Portman and published as *Animals At Risk: Whales in Danger*. All new material in this edition is authored by Tricia Hoffman.

Editor: Tricia Hoffman
Book Design: Beeline Media and Design

Photo Credits: Cover, p. 1 Maui Topical Images/Shutterstock.com; p. 5 Earth theater/Shutterstock.com; p. 6 Alexander Baumann/Shutterstock.com; p. 7 Delz76/Shutterstock.com; p. 9 Ajit S N/Shutterstock.com; p. 10 Jody Ann/Shutterstock.com; p. 11 Will Falcon/Shutterstock.com; p. 13 GUDKOV ANDREY/Shutterstock.com; p. 14 TSViPhoto/Shutterstock.com; p. 15 James C Farr/Shutterstock.com; p. 17 ChameleonsEye/Shutterstock.com; p. 18 GreenOak/Shutterstock.com; p. 19 ArtDary/Shutterstock.com; p. 20 Mikadun/Shutterstock.com; p. 21 Camcp/Shutterstock.com; p. 21 dee karen/Shutterstock.com; p. 21 Pictandra/Shutterstock.com; p. 21 Pau Venteo/Shutterstock.com

Cataloging-in-Publication Data
Names: Hoffman, Tricia.
Title: Whales / Tricia Hoffman.
Description: Buffalo, New York : PowerKids Press, 2027. | Series: Edge of extinction | Includes glossary and index.
Identifiers: ISBN 9781499457988 (pbk.) | ISBN 9781499457995 (library bound) | ISBN 9781499458008 (ebook)
Subjects: LCSH: Whales--Juvenile literature. | Whales--Conservation--Juvenile literature.
Classification: LCC QL737.C4 H644 2027 | DDC 599.5--dc23

Printed in China

CPSIA Compliance Information: Batch #QSPK27. For Further Information contact Rosen Publishing at 1-800-237-9932.

# Contents



Words in the glossary appear in **bold** type the first time they are used in the text.

# Meet the Whale

Whales swim through all five of the world's oceans. But they aren't fish—they're **mammals**. Unlike fish, whales must swim to the surface to breathe air.

Whales, along with dolphins and **porpoises**, belong to a group of animals called cetaceans. There are about 90 **species** of cetaceans.

Six whale species are currently **endangered**. Unless people take action, they may become **extinct** and die out completely.

**ON THE EDGE**

Whale species are divided into two groups: toothed whales and baleen whales.

All cetaceans have sleek bodies that easily glide through water.

# Whales with Teeth

Killer whales, or orcas, are toothed whales. So are dolphins and porpoises. As their name suggests, toothed whales have teeth. Toothed whales eat fish, squid, octopus, and other sea animals.

Whales can't breathe through their mouth. Toothed whales have an opening on top of their head called a blowhole. They use these blowholes to breathe. The blowhole opens to allow air into and out of the whale's lungs. This allows the whale to breathe while swimming.

**ON THE EDGE**

Most toothed whales are smaller than baleen whales.

The sperm whale is the largest toothed whale. It can grow to be 60 feet (18 m) long.

# Whales with Baleen

Humpback whales are baleen whales. So are blue whales. Baleen whales get their name from comb-like plates called baleen in their mouth. These plates are made of the same matter our fingernails are. Most baleen whales feed by taking big gulps of water and using the baleen to remove sea creatures, such as **krill** and small fish, from the water.

Blue whales are the largest of all whales. They are possibly the largest animal to have ever lived on Earth. They can grow to more than 100 feet (30 m) long and weigh as much as 200 tons (181 t). The sounds they make are some of the loudest of any animal.

**ON THE EDGE**

Baleen whales have two blowholes.

A blue whale's tongue is so big that an elephant could stand on it.

# Echolocation

Toothed whales make sounds that bounce off underwater objects. The whales use the **echoes** to find food and to avoid danger. This is called **echolocation**. Echolocation is especially useful in dark and cloudy water where whales can't see well.

Scientists don't think baleen whales use echolocation. However, humpback whales make sounds called whale songs. They probably sing to let other whales know they're nearby.

**ON THE EDGE**

Whales have good eyesight and excellent hearing.

Toothed whales live in large groups called pods. This helps with protection and hunting.

# Illegal Whaling

For hundreds of years, humans have hunted whales for their blubber, baleen, and meat. Whale fat, called blubber, was used to make soap and oil for lamps and candles. Baleen was used to make products such as tennis rackets, umbrellas, and hats. Today, whale hunting is mostly for the animals' meat.

Hunting whales, or whaling, is now illegal in most countries. However, people in countries such as Japan, Iceland, and Norway continue to hunt whales. It is **estimated** that nearly 40,000 large whales have been killed in these three countries in the past 40 years.

**ON THE EDGE**

More than 100,000 small whales, dolphins, and porpoises are killed each year.

Some species of whales can live up to 100 years or more.

# Pollution in the Water

Pollution is another risk to whales in the wild. Dangerous **chemicals** and metals make their way into the oceans. Some are dumped into the water. Some leak into the ground and then spread from the ground into the ocean. Small amounts of toxic chemicals can end up in the sea creatures that are eaten by whales. Since whales eat such large amounts of food, dangerous amounts of those chemicals can build up in their bodies. The metal mercury, for example, does great harm to mammals' brains. It can hurt their chances of having babies.

Humpback whales migrate each year. They feed in cold waters and give birth in warm waters. Whales traveling between Alaska and Hawaii can cover the 3,000-mile (4,800-km) distance in 36 days.

# Ship Strikes and Bycatch

Every day, ships travel the world's oceans. Unfortunately, these ships sometimes hit whales. Fast-moving boats can seriously hurt or even kill whales. In addition, the noise made by boat traffic is loud and can confuse them. Since many whales depend on echolocation to find food, noise from boats can scare them away from feeding areas.

Fishing nets can catch whales by mistake. This is called bycatch. When a whale gets twisted in a fishing net and can't come to the surface for air, it drowns. Nets can also get wrapped around a whale's mouth so it can't eat. It is estimated that 300,000 whales and dolphins are killed each year because of bycatch.

**ON THE EDGE**

Ships are the cause of an estimated 90 percent of the deaths of young Northern right whales.

Thousands of whales are killed or injured each year after being struck by ships.

# Dangerous Drilling

Oil drilling poses dangers to whales and their food supplies. Underwater explosions are used in building oil wells. These noises can severely harm a whale's hearing. Since whales depend so much on their hearing, this can change their lives and put them in danger.

Sometimes, oil accidentally leaks into the ocean. This is called an oil spill. If a whale surfaces in water covered with oil, it can suck the toxic oil into its lungs. Oil can plug its blowhole, making it hard or impossible for the whale to breathe. Oil spills can also poison or kill the whales' food supply.

Gray whales travel more than 12,000 miles (19,300 km) as they swim from Alaska to Mexico and back each year.

# Save the Whales!

Whales face a variety of dangers in the wild. Fortunately, many groups are working with governments around the world to stop pollution, improve oil-drilling safety, and end whaling. They hope these efforts, along with many others, will save whales.

Luckily, **conservation** efforts seem to be working. Gray whales were once near extinction, but their numbers have increased in recent years. Everyone can work together to help save the whales—and that means you can help too!

**ON THE EDGE**

Female whales give birth to only a few babies in their lifetime. This means that it can take a long time for a whale population to grow.

# What Can You Do to Help?

Sing to Save The Whales Day is May 15th. It teaches people about the importance of whales and the dangers they face. Write a song to encourage people to protect marine life.

Don't let balloons fly away. Helium balloons can travel far and wind up in the ocean. This can hurt many ocean animals, including whales and the animals they eat.

Reduce, reuse, and recycle as much as you can. Making small changes will decrease pollution and help save the whales and their habitats.

Teach others. Tell friends and family members what you've learned about whales and how they can help save them too.

# Glossary

**chemical:** matter that can be mixed with other matter to cause changes

**conservation:** the care of the natural world

**echo:** a sound that repeats because it bounces off an object

**echolocation:** a way of locating objects with echoes

**endangered:** in danger of dying out

**estimated:** describing a guess based on knowledge or facts

**extinct:** having no living members

**krill:** a tiny ocean creature that looks like a shrimp

**mammal:** an animal that has live young and feeds them milk from the mother's body

**porpoise:** a toothed sea mammal that has a rounded nose and a triangular fin

**species:** a group of animals that are all of the same kind

# Fact Check

1. How many blowholes do toothed whales have?
   a. one b. two c. three
2. Humpback whales and blue whales are ______ whales.
   a. toothed b. baleen c. gray
3. What is a group of whales called?
   a. a krill b. a blubber c. a pod

Answers: 1. a, 2. b, 3. c

# On the Internet

**Whale**
*https://animals.sandiegozoo.org/animals/whale*
Read facts about the lives of whales and hear what a humpback whale sounds like!

**Whale Facts**
*www.worldwildlife.org/species/whale*
Learn what's being done to save whales.

**Publisher's note to educators and parents:** Our editors have carefully reviewed these websites to ensure that they are suitable for students. Many websites change frequently, however, and we cannot guarantee that a site's future contents will continue to meet our high standards of quality and educational value. Be advised that students should be closely supervised whenever they access the Internet.

# Index